LIAR, LIAR, LICK, SPIT

Also by Emma Neale

Novels
Night Swimming (Vintage, 1998)
Little Moon (Vintage, 2001)
Double Take (Vintage, 2003)
Relative Strangers (Vintage, 2006)
Fosterling (Vintage, 2011)
Billy Bird (Vintage, 2016)

Poetry
Sleeve-notes (Godwit, 1999)
How to Make a Million (Godwit, 2002)
Spark (Steele Roberts, 2008)
The Truth Garden (Otago University Press, 2012)
Tender Machines (Otago University Press, 2015)
To the Occupant (Otago University Press, 2019)

Short fiction
The Pink Jumpsuit (Quentin Wilson Publishing, 2021)

Liar, Liar, Lick, Spit
Emma Neale

OTAGO UNIVERSITY PRESS
Te Whare Tā o Ōtākou Whakaihu Waka

Liar, liar, lick spit
turn about the candlestick.

— from a playground rhyme

CONTENTS

7	False Confession
9	Porky
10	Spare Change
12	The Quiet Type
14	A Very *Perhaps* Man
15	In the nodding grass below the cat's-cradle clothesline, my hand an open perch
16	Like girls were hot soft scones
18	Tyranny
20	Split Decision
21	Mask
22	Pandora First Gets Feminism, Age Ten
23	Pre-teen
24	&
25	Threat
27	Horn
29	Found
31	Torque/Talk
32	Like the albums on rotate in your first year away from home
33	The Barnum Effect
34	The Piano Tuner
35	Terribly Involved
37	The Lake
38	Wanting to believe in the butterfly effect
40	Arrhythmia
41	Androphobia
43	A general concurrence about the consequences of identity theft, falsified qualifications and culpable negligence
45	Player

46	Night-call
48	Little Fibs
49	⌘S
50	Sleepless
51	My Blank Camouflage
53	Scapegoat
54	Tricks of Trade
55	Genealogy
59	#notmetoothanks
61	Histology Report
64	The Moth-eyed Steeplechase Horse
66	The Night Shift
68	If you saw a miracle, would you speak of it?
70	Wishing he'd declined cocktails, stayed at home to read Janet Frame
72	Stranded
74	'Just the plain truth, as only a liar can tell it'
76	*Sempre marcatissimo*
78	Dreams are the dark glasses and heatproof shell the mind wears when the truth is a hot, burning ball of plasma and at least sixty-seven known elements
80	An Abraham Darby Rose

*

85	The Lie's Version

*

87	Notes & Acknowledgements

False Confession

For Kurdish poet İlhan Sami Çomak

If you beat a man
hard enough
he'll say anything

admit he set fire
to the forests above the city
when there are no forests
above his city

agree the scars
left on his neck,
the ache in his shoulders,
are from some boyhood joy curtailed:
a flight on horseback,
a swing so high it nearly let
his street-dusty shoe tips
double-tap the rooftops —
abrupted by a tumble, a sickening crack.

And yet it makes them uneasy, doesn't it —
those nameless thugs, power's hired goons —
his recall of the *before*, so vivid, so accurate?
The way the starlight, the peppery scent
of earth, grass, the night breeze sleek as a caracal,
still rise in him, seem to lift him elsewhere

even now his convictions
are broadcast like a mist of pollen
that drifts and soaks into the mind's ink

as it wells and spills from this foreign pen
16,590 kilometres across the oceans, the continents
and the forests, bristling green, song cacophonous,
that lift above this city, as solid as eyewitnesses.

Porky

'The real history of consciousness starts with one's first lie.' — *Joseph Brodsky*

The time I told my grandmother that rare treat, a school lunch order, had never arrived: it was a *porky* indeed, for mine was pure greed. I thought Gran wouldn't feed me her cloud-puff scones if she knew I'd scoffed the entire fish and chip feast. But my tale trapped her in the trouble of embarrassment.

She phoned the school to complain. 'You must be mistaken,' the secretary laughed. She had seen me clutch the steamy, paper-swathed bundle, unwrap it like I'd won pass the parcel, and devour every morsel. Under lunchtime sun the oily salt on my hands shone glossy as beads on a princess dress. I licked my fingers, pink tip by pink tip.

Does your mouth water, too, even now, with words like *secret, full, wanted, happy*?

But moments after I recall those chips and my new labels, *greedy, piggy, fibber*, I realise my first memory of a lie is a lie.

Reaching back to years before, I remember how in a quiet house, my mother heard the baby cry out from deep sleep inside the crib.

I stood by the cot, denial and contrition struggling inside me like demon and angel too colossal to hold inside my skin. My mother — my Good Witch Glinda — asked calmly, 'What happened?'

I looked to the air, looked behind us, looked between the bars of the cot. 'A ghost hit her,' I answered.

The punishment descended. '*I don't believe you, Emma.*'

My name paled into phantom, ghoul, shameful synonym for *stranger*. I felt my presence thin and thin, as the dear, chubby baby was lifted into our mother's arms.

Spare Change

New to London, maybe I gave off the scent Naïve
to the ragged man who shuffled

along the tube train aisle
where I stood gripping the pole

amid the massed bodies of rush-hour crush;
each face, it seemed, averted in disgust.

Like the small-town citizen I really was
when the man said, 'Can you help me, love?'

I met his gaze then looked down
to see what he wanted to show me:

his forearm split open, swollen,
infection swarming like red wasps.

'I need some change to get to hospital.
Spare a couple of quid?'

I didn't know local custom. How to draw a blank
down over the mind, or how to give a pound

as indifferently as if our hands held slots for cash.
Instead I cried out, 'What happened to you? Oh my God.'

He stalled, his stare a flame held too close,
then rolled down shirt and jacket sleeves.

'Never mind.' He pushed through the throng
as our train hurtled to the next stop.

A second stranger tapped my shoulder.
'Forget him. He's a con artist.'

But the fire-swarmed gash.
The pomegranate gasp of it.

The man shrugged. 'Doesn't let it heal.
I've seen him. Uses pocket knives, tin lids.

Grifter. Scabber. Shows wounds for sympathy.
Don't encourage him with money.'

One man so strung out he'd self-harm for cash.
Another so jaded he'd cauterised compassion.

Decades on, the memory opens
and reopens in the same raw place.

As if I could heal anything
as pernicious as indifference

I am at it again with the saline and sutures
of these ink-black glyphs

needle and stitch
needle and stitch.

The Quiet Type

The strangest lie
I ever told as a child
left me cornered.
I was six. Maybe five.

We were on the mat at music time.
A boy behind me droned
like a bee in tin headphones.
I squirmed and turned around.
My mute, dark look meant
Try a little piece of quiet.

The teacher stopped the whole class.
'Emma,' she said.
'What did you just do?'

I told a true untruth:
'I said to sing more softly.'
I'd thought it; wanted it;
hadn't spoken a word of it.

Did I think that she'd agree?
Detect some musical gift,
admonish the glared-at child,
'Sing in key'?

Or did I think she could, like a god,
see each of my thoughts
as if my head was a shoebox,
all my deeds and errors
like shadow puppets

of crimes and *oughts*
in a diorama of gold foil,
black sugar paper, cherry cellophane?

In a lesson I now take to mean
it is often best to keep one's own counsel
I was sent to stand, face to the wall
beside the rubbish bin,
its rotten-fruit smell of sin
strong as the taste of shame:
this sour ash I still can't spit.

A Very *Perhaps* Man

As a child when she could be sure
her mother wouldn't ride the anger horse
she liked to play little elegant afternoons.
The sun took her in tiny stinging bites
as she sat quietly with her thin plastic dolls,
role models of pink glow and hollow serene
while a mirror noticed her father's slippers
fill with shadows.
Yes, he was always
a very *perhaps* man
at work late even on Sundays
wearing his handsome talent out.

In the nodding grass below the cat's-cradle clothesline, my hand an open perch

It didn't seem to me that　　I　　had anything pitted and rotten in my heart
when I was six and　　asked　　the universe if a bird could please meet me
in my hand's root-white arc.　　God　　-like, my 'Let one land' — was that the error?
Bidding the sweetness come near?　　If　　it had kissed its feathers
into the scoop-bone nest of me,　　I　　would have transfigured how,
did I believe?　　Could　　it, in truth, have brought slow-burn disaster
if I'd been allowed to　　carry　　the papery claws, velvet scuffle, small heart's indicator
blip-blop-blipping like　　a　　signal that I could turn the world to my whims?
As if others' lives, fate, were　　sparrow　　-light playthings, expendable trinkets,
my love ersatz, sentimental, as any　　fledgling　　oppressor's.

Like girls were hot soft scones

For Emer Lyons

At Sunday School, I always felt bad for Adam —
God taking away his rib like that.
The hurt must have been worse
than the time I dislocated my toes
and Dad wrenched back
their weird new burning hooks
into their sockets again.
Even that agony meant zilch
when I tripped and truly broke
the same two toes only moments later —
what great pain could come from such small things!

So imagine Adam, lying there, dusty tan,
like a man buried to his neck in beach sand,
only he was the sand, a Sandman waking
out of God's dream of having someone to show His tricks to:
then, poor man, having a deep part of him removed
as if now God thought cutting a live body
was just a children's game of Operation —
how could you do that to someone you loved,
even to give them company? Would I have given a rib
to help make Jeffrey, or Darryl? The boys down the road
who after school walked me home, invited me to tinker
with offcuts, nails, coping saws, make swords
like wonky crosses, any misfire with a hammer
that blued a thumb enough to make all three of us cry?

Well, would I?
My stomach ached with questions the Bible raised.
Church people thought girls were like hot soft scones
and Sunday School teachers were the glinting blades
avid to fillet us, spread blame like seed-pitted jam
gritty and sticky on our skins — but why feel responsible
for what Adam had lost, what Eve had done?

If I took a pinch from a playdough man
to make a playdough woman
they smelled, tasted, squashed back down the same.
Weren't they both just clay? Tangy, salty, equal clay?
If Eve was cursed to have her sorrow multiplied,
always to be dissatisfied, did the rope of *not fair*
that coiled round my chest mean God was one big long
nyah nyah, told you so?

I hadn't stolen the apple, neither had my mum.
Nor my baby sister, nor any of the girls at school,
not even the ones in lace-topped socks I was jealous of.
God was overreacting. He needed to be sent outside,
put on His own back doorstep, so He could see
skinny spiders practise cartwheels on the concrete,
ladybirds lift their red ponchos to show black satin,
cabbage moths dock the tiny white yachts of themselves
in the quiet green bay of a leaf — so He could, from that place,
like the kitchen radio sang, *look down on Creation* —
feel His rage dissipate into the sunny butter-melt of calm,
still the closest thing to heaven we have found.

Tyranny

I first met the latest despot
when we were nine:
he was red-haired, freckled,
on my team in some indoors ball game
when I fumbled one near catch.

His index finger jabbed,
puncturing the sweat-hung air.
His face so raw and peeled with anger
I saw thoughts could make a mind chafe and blister
as he yelled

'You fat *bitch*,
you *shit* for brains
you piece of *crap*,
you *loser*,'

and though surrounded
by other children
and the teacher,
I was afraid —
not so very much of him
(for *fat bitch*:
I had the size advantage)

but of what hidden thing
had happened to him;
was still happening,
somewhere, to him
because of *do unto others*

as you would have them
do unto you.

What I feared was
if someone breaks
the gentle chain of care,
what next? Who mends it?
What else might the split links do
as they dangle alone in space?

However I worded it then —
might that bully go to prison one day?
If everyone does an unto
to someone
how do we undo each one? —

it was the kind of enquiry
I was told I was still
far too young
to bother with,
which, hindsight says,
was yet another of the adults'
strange, ritual untruths

for there I was:
bothering with it,
proof that each time
the mind is wounded
it learns new
and darker repertoires.

Split Decision

When my mother asked my father
to cut down on his long hours

but he wouldn't; when she asked him if he could at least
tell her that their relationship still came first

he was honest, principled and upright —
where perhaps he might have saved their marriage

with a loving
bridal white lie.

Mask

If every fiction tells a secret
without revealing it,
if it both dispels and creates
a little more mystery
than exists
before it unravels
like red flame that frets
through white wax paper
that conceals an aniseed sweet,
let me here confess
the worst deception
I ever committed
I entered into unwillingly
in that, from the moment
an infant first discovers
the power in a mock cry,
it is given
a false identity
as witness protection
from which the only release
will be as on a stage set
when a cloak swirls
to reveal
a dropped mask
rocking gently
to and fro on the floorboards
like an empty rowboat
ghosting with a diver's spring,
now moored and
lit by silence.

Pandora First Gets Feminism, Age Ten

The first time Pandora's parents left her alone, hunger to know … *anything* flickered in her ribs, like a firefly in a paragon jar, lighting the way with its small torch song.

The house turned treasure hunt. Cupboards and closets explored, Pandora's hands darted over skirts, scarves; her mother's wardrobe a walled garden whispering woodsy, citrusy scents. Her father's bureau was grim with receipts, the blind worms of socks, his twin brushes gritted together: one for each unruly side of the Einstein *sproing!* of the hair he'd wet and scrape, scrape, like the razor punishing his face, forbidding natural disorder.

All this was too familiar. Bored, Pandora lay on the floor; which is how she found the magazines stowed below her father's bedside, their images of naked women in slave collars and chains; of giant cakes shaped like *private places*; more photos of women stretched out like languid cats or skinny rotisserie chickens, their breasts stark as peeled eggs inside bikini burn-lines. She found, too, a story of the perfect wife: she who had athletic sex, gave birth, then vanished, leaving the 'baby' — a sports car — for her man.

Pandora slammed the magazines shut — glow of curiosity doused. But the imps and hobgoblins were out: confusion; a hot humiliation; the sore, whorled colours of *injustice* almost too clogged and injurious for words.

Yet Pandora charged her dad, point blank, with the facts: *I found your magazines.* He protested, sheepish as a child: *I'm sorry. I didn't want them. My friends made me take them.* And so, Hope straggled in, carried on the part gladness, part promise that there was in learning her father was never really a god.

Pre-teen

'Truth is twelve years old' — *Goan proverb*

She's walking up the gravel strip
beside the grassy berm
along the coastal street
barefoot, blue jeans,
cicadas electric in the hedge
stuck like a bad garage band
thrashing on their few chords
she's jaunty with sea salt
beachy sweat in her pits
a swipe of sand on her jaw
like her dad's holiday stubble
and she whistles to the finches
that wheel up from the paddock hay,
chaws on a piece of soldier grass
with its micro-corona of white petals
swaggers, mind flexing,
muscles imagining
nobody's body
but her bones'

&

For Poppy Haynes

I know some
can't stand
the ampersand
yet when I see
its curled strand
I remember cellos,
a cellist & the small
upflick flourish
of a finale bow stroke,
the way the coiled thread
mirrors a G clef's slopes,
so now & then
I try its loose slipknot
which seems to tie
a contented, ready
tone to the page:
a little like the note
you hear
when a young
cellist's mother
bends above
a borrowed pair
of shiny, lace-up
recital shoes
while she hums
first we do
this loop
&
then we do
this one too

Threat

The school bell shrieks its chalk
down the daylight's spine.
Is this a drill, can you smell smoke?
No need to.
It already clouds the teachers' faces.
The silence around the alarm's
frantic hammer and anvil
says this is no rehearsal.
The staff are a paradox,
gentle riot squad
who barely exchange looks.
'Move, girls. Now. *Move*.'

We're quick; we're orderly;
we ditch our bags and books,
soon gather in the quadrangle,
fish for shooting in a barrel.

The sunshine knows how to do surreal.
It touches each one of us on the crown:
black and blonde and red and brown
all gilded. It lifts a blue blur-like aura
around even the bitches' shoulders,
gives their white school shirts
the Persil elegance of swans.
Every one of us is illuminated
into something brighter
more urgent than beautiful:
for now we catch the acrid rumour
that spurts like flame along fuse-wire

bomb threat

we swallow with tongues like flour
we breathe through throats like paper
we shift on our cattle-truck haunches
as like jet fighters in formation
all the dread and sadness roar over —

someone mentions Libya
someone mentions their father
who thins with terminal cancer
another mentions their mother
who night-walks too young in dementia
another says a boy has molested her
so now she can't keep down what she eats
another's dreams of nuclear fallout
mean she hardly ever sleeps.

As we stand there the winch
of patience winds higher
tense with expectation
of thunder
shatter
sirens
fire

yet there is no bomb

and still we could never call this a *hoax*:
for even now we carry
the solid strop of time
the knife that whets and whets,
and gripped inside our chests
a red grenade of fear.

Horn

The boys in the park
outside my son's first kung fu class
boot a football about
with voices that wheeze like glitchy doorbells,
rusted harmonicas soaked in flaming Sambuca,
crude buzzers for *you lose* on quiz shows.

They quack and bark *fuck* and *cunt*
relentless as roosters on crack
while they hurl around a girl's name
as if it too is made of fake leather,
pumped with giddy, glassy air,
and which, when they aim it, just won't go there:
it zips skyward at crazy angles,
bounds off the goal posts, races into traffic.

The very fact of her, somewhere in the world,
makes them bellow like the baby bull, chained to a fence,
that kept us awake all night through altitude headaches
in Nepal, its hollow midnight groans enough to make
my young husband vow that in the morning
he'd give up vegetarianism for good —

though he never did — and when I remember
how he couldn't quit his own essential gentleness
it softens me to these nearly-men
(though I grit my ears' tiny watchwork bones
against their honk, and cuss, and drone):
they must suffer in their own raw joints,
their straining skins,
a little like that poor calf did,

lashed to a stake, iron ring through its nose
black as mushroom gills, velvet as Diwali marigolds,
with the tight, cramped zing of unborn joy in its ball sack,
the low, clotted moan jammed in its throat
a half-moon lump of sour milk, hard as a hoof;
that young animal at once striving for speech
and flailing from it
yet in that urgent captive
battered trombone bray
articulating so much
of what our bodies
go on wanting
and wanting to say.

Found

At the end of a sunny parquet corridor:
the odd shock of mud dumped
on its pristine polished floor.

Closer in, vision adjusts;
the lump becomes a salt-rasp sob
that clots the building's throat.

Dread-dense as a sea mine,
heavy as a bell cut dumb,
little ditched anchor of *gone away*,

a baby curls on its knees, sleep-sunk,
as if in air's last sweet underlayer
as the planet burns.

No eyes, but it sucks a thumb
that our own tongues know
would give the blunt tang

of the jungle bars we licked at school,
a taste like the salted plum
of lips split by a swing's chain links.

This earth-brown lostling
is a cast taken of grief's naked wail,
the raw howl of denial

of the void space
in a child's form
that makes a *vilomah*.

It's all I can do not to clutch his dark ice limbs
to breasts that sting with milk's phantom,
drawn as if I'm his alloy, part him;

all I can do not to rock and cry
as when my own sons made day break
with the red-hot radicles of their spines

that shed me — peach flesh parted on stone,
agate cored with fire — as together we strove
for them both to enter

the shape and light of their names
that seem to open now
in love's translations
for *keep*, for *found*.

Torque/Talk

What if that thing that happened to you once
What if that sudden torque and sear and clench
What if that thing that seemed to go under
swallowed by air as if by water
bewilderingly invisible so soon after
What if that thing meant you were changed forever?
Strange aversions, abrupt paralysis, panic swarms amassing in the mind's caverns[†]
though there were days when you could say
I'm one of the luckiest people alive;
days when you could say *and I know*
I don't even know how lucky or alive I truly am

† Beneath the skin, the train of the incident. Say one carriage collapsed and telescoped, another like the body of a woman contorted in an S-bend as she cranes away, resists a sudden heavy shunting compression. Say for the sake of this comparison, it lies akin to the splintered wood the bent steel the broken seats the eyes the hair follicles the smoke of clove cigarettes the flawed auditory nerves the thrust the apple-cider tongue of the driver, let's call him the driver, in the aftermath, the new collision of the explanatory late-night visit, another kind of moral stain the slow silent chemical leach of it into the very still, very placid, very numb blue lake waters.

Like the albums on rotate in your first year away from home

He didn't ever love her
the way she wanted to be loved
but he kept her first letters
inside a concertina file that held
a polished spiral shell
a wooden comb painted
with a heron-white-faced woman
in a scarlet kimono;
discontinued coins, keys to forgotten flats,
and written on the backs of concert tickets
things she'd said beside the docks
where her lips and eyelids glittered
like sealight chiselled by the frost,
things that rang still in his memory
like tenets, truths to live by
so at fifty, through the brandy
and then the whisky
and then the midnight bitter ice-field
of a working dad's insomnia
he had to wonder, he wondered
as the years came surging forward
why they couldn't take him with them,
couldn't take him with them.

The Barnum Effect

On a deserted early London morning,
the footpaths skate-rink shiny with dawn rain,
an older man called to me from under shop awnings.

He sashayed, swept off his hat, clasped it to his chest.
'An angel with a broken wing,' he sang.
All I gave was a grin, a quick duck of the head,

the shape of my back from the fast clip
that women are taught says self-possession,
wary, through experience, of men too smooth or flip

and of my own pulse's helter-skelter,
swooping heedlessly
to a crooner's synthetic nectar.

Yet in a particular terracotta autumn light
that ten-second suitor-stranger
still sometimes comes to mind

his tone as if he knew me as soon as he saw me —
although if he understood precisely
how to make swoon with the song of *anybody*

I think he also sang mostly,
if slantwise,
of himself.

The Piano Tuner

Every spring he returns, shuts all our doors and windows
so that berry-drunk, egg-plump birdsong

can't spill bright raucous stains through the air
while he tests whether each key still prints

its crisp, open note
on the unfolded folio of silence.

The click and clatter of his tools
when he picks them up, sets them aside,

sound like tape measure, scissors, quick unpick,
as if he cuts, pins and hand-stitches

a bespoke, swallow-tailed coat
which he slips into as he begins

to play this brief and broken
annual concerto:

scales and arpeggios that leak free
all of life; its gather, rise and falter

before the single, velveted clap
of a varnished wooden lid.

Terribly Involved

I lay there at night next to our son's hospital bed
his small, warm hand in mine
while in the next bay along another child cried.
Empty chairs sat vigil at his side.
Safe after surgery, our son slept, if fitfully;
that nine-month-old baby, not at all.

His wail was so desolate and cold
I saw an image from a long-forgotten film:
a blind Arctic fox cub trotted along ice
that broke and calved so a small floe
carried it into open ocean.

I slipped out to stand by the metal cot
near the baby in his nest of tubes and needles.
Hush, hush, little one, I whispered, *hey, hey, little baby.*
His cry swelled, fell like snow.
I called for the night nurse, asked,
Can I pick the baby up when you're busy, is it safe to hold him?

Best not, she said. *The parents might not approve.*
Half afraid to hear, I asked, *Where are they?*
At home, she answered. *They're just not terribly involved.*

I tried to find shock, judgement
in the grim brackets of her mouth;
to cling on to her choice: *terribly*,
but saw the practised calm of her face
just meant she'd seen far worse.

I thought of our own first maternity nurse
the platitudes trotted out, blithe as free brochures:
Babies bring all the love they need.
News headlines said the opposite.
What about the neglected, I'd asked, *the abandoned?*
Her reply: *Their souls are on a journey, to atone for past lives.*

Fictions she told her clients, not feeling they were lies?
Homilies to keep herself coming to her job
where she saw miseries she couldn't repair
even if she could say, *Hush, hush, little one*;
even if she could, once a fortnight, then once a month
for a designated time, lift each baby up,
give them, briefly, all the love they came to bear.

The Lake

This child feels it like blue pollen that makes her hive of fingers dance.
This one a groove along his spine that must be filled with running.
Another as music that only rises here, deep in his mind, never sung.
This last, as crystal numbers that link, fold and fall like pleats in time.

We think they all must know the lake's mother tongue.
They are her water cupped in our hands,
new skins for the old light we believed in.

Wanting to believe in the butterfly effect

I collect a box of groceries from cold storage,
take it to the welfare centre, break open bread rolls

fill them with salad, cheese, mayonnaise, leave goofy notes
about the extra cucumber for beauty treatment, or vegans,

in the hope that kindness migrates invisible currents
to pollinate every tyrant's heart —

They feel their hearts!

While our children, whom we had for love of the world,
watch polar ice caps collapse on TV; say with furious fluency

sixth mass extinction, eyes the soot of burnt-out stumps.
They walk to school all weathers, forgo meat and dairy food,

kneel in postures half bereft, half hopeful,
as we press thin seedling roots like a cluster of skinny wires

into the rich dark sockets of a field's edge, afraid even planting trees
might be superstitious as *cross your heart and hope to die*,

fingers kissed to single magpies,
green dresses forbidden on first-time brides.

Our sons help us squash the sluggy pearls of grass grubs
that would eat the seedlings before they grow

but as fire blackens the planet's treasure map
one son asks, in a toneless blank,

'Why do people even have children?'
The youngest hugs me, his body's slim shuttle

shaking with the gravity of the mind's strain.
'You shouldn't have had us, Mum.'

But we had you because we loved the world.

Stern young faces gavel-blunt, their twinned silences
sentence us as yet more militants of doublespeak.

In order to show our love for the planet,
we had children who could grieve for it.

Arrhythmia

The young house surgeon
jogs the tree-canopied avenue

blue earphones hutched
in his ears, pink iPod clutched

in a fist he holds a little aloft,
as he presses that small metal song-box

against the air's clammy ribs
expression abstracted yet intent

as if he's never not on shift
and with the smallest of stethoscopes

auscultates the epoch's
serious irregularities.

Androphobia

It begins when the child finds deceit
turns to truth if certain adults use it.
His tongue still curls at the grit of wrong,
like it did at the crumbs stuck to the sweets
from that man's jacket pockets.

I don't like that maths teacher.
He puts his hands down my pants.
He tries to make me forget
by giving me lollies.
I don't want them, either.

His parents inform the school.
No speech, no ceremony,
the teacher disappears.
Yet the principal, for four more years,
singles out the child for humiliation:
says he is dishonest, filthy minded, a failure.
Sometimes it almost seems correct.
For the boy slips his parents the tale
that school is 'much better now',
although, like grime under fingernails,
the man's repeated act is lodged in his head.
Each time he recalls it, a muddy tide
rises in his mind and he forgets
so much else: capitals, verbs, his sums.
It is so hard, to retain the worth of things
when the value of one is thought greater than another,
and yet that one, the one always called
a brilliant educator,
seemed to believe mint or barley sugar

would heal the ice-pick split
that touch left in the mind,
would nullify the fear of men.

A general concurrence about the consequences of identity theft, falsified qualifications and culpable negligence

When we found out about the men
who said they had done
what they hadn't done
and who said they were
who they weren't
the sensation was
like the rotation of a barrel
a twisting and a wrenching
a rocking back and forth
it was a trembling and a shaking and a twisting
a sudden lurching and a mother who said
she felt like she was being tilted over backwards
it was a sister who began to shiver without respite
she said, as the eye is still her witness, it was
feeling a dreadful heading-down like being on a slope
where the sliding would not stop
and the next sensation came in stages
there was a very wrong feeling of an ending with a jolt
but soon a wave of not wanting the way
the room was being sucked in and down,
and down, and down,
because reality was crumbling very fast
it looked like mist began to gather in
but it was coming from the ground
and there was more swaying and a thought of forward-falling
as reality and disbelief slam-dunked into themselves
the top floated earthwards the rest exploded outwards
shattered into a sinkhole and was devoured by the dust
and then the next sensation was as if a husband and a father

dropped to the floor and looked across to see another
whose hands were outstretched above their head
vanishing from sight and then all of us saw
the truth sway west and there was
a very short time when the initial violent twisting
seemed to pause and the crowd of us
heard a rumbling which made us look up
and that was the moment
when we witnessed
the final story collapse.

Player

It is not complete deception when he says
he's having coffee today with an old school friend.
There will be coffee, perhaps a maple and ginger muffin;
there will be a companion, seated across from him.
They will talk, face and hands in neutral; there will be no touch.

But in his chest, throat, the soft hollows of his arms and legs,
a chaotic tumult as all the cells contract, contort,
strive to reform as xylem, phloem, chlorophyll,
the lie, all the lies in him thickening like Pinocchio's ridiculous nose,
pushing their dreadful woody stalks and clarinet-mouthed flowers out,

out, on to his tongue, numbing his lips, making him sick, showing his complicity
although today he hasn't said, or done, anything of consequence —
it's just that she sits there, the trust in her smile as clear
as if she's shown a sucked sweet gripped between white teeth
and he forgets which untruth he has spun for whom.

His heart pounds, fox bayed at through the dark bars
of each bluff's thickened and tangled branches.
Predator and prey, he lies in wait.

Night-call

When the day he died
turned its face away
and became our night

sleep was severed like a cord.
We wandered a circuit of streets
wintered in a dark so deep

we felt spun in a wave of ice.
Tar-black footpath and inkwell sky
tumbled and swung in a chill swoop.

Unknit night, unstrung sun, noon-star moon,
what measure, what world, what news was this
where the heart could slit

like a full new sack of crystal grain
caught on a metal hook
and when from the witch-claw reach

of our landlord's front-yard tree
that in six years had never borne
a single green-winged leaf,

a solitary bird could suddenly sing and sing
a star-beaded embroidery in triplets rising?
Melody so Mozartian, sweet-fibred,

it capsized the senses,
wrote bioluminescence in audio,
a sung italics of wrongness, confusion,

the wrench and lean
of an omen delivered so late
it was no longer an omen.

Death to breath,
night to day, song to sob,
half orphan or daughter

the scarring disquiet
of that night lark's weird beauty
is the sparkle of glass
still lipped by a wound.

Little Fibs

Let us praise
the small evasions:
the missed call
the slight sore throat
the prior engagement;
the short works of fiction
that act like the turn of a key,
the snib of a front door's fly screen
which mean we can try to forge the silence
that ferries us to the hinterland of the wildest interior.

⌘S

I kept your texts.
They shine, fire axes
behind finger-printed glass.

Sleepless

In midnight's cold quarter
I woke with my mouth full
of a half-lost song's opening.
It began with your name, so for a moment
the collapse in time was less terrifying,
as when a Greek goddess of something good,
like a clean moon unsheathed, rises opposite,
snakes trapped, live knives, in her fists,
blades blunting in her blood's heat,
her bared breasts worn as calmly
as a wild pear tree its opal drupes.
The havoc of fears dimmed,
the wind making small moan
like gratefulness in an unseen animal's throat,
the night sky outside as drusy with stars
as the static electricity I once saw crackle
from your arms raised in deep winter
as we unfastened fast in the banked-up dark.

My Blank Camouflage

Where did I learn it, the trick that saved me?
It wasn't whispered by my mother,
it wasn't mimed by my sister,
slipping back from night stops and star-snap alleys
where she'd learnt the secret from other girls,
black eyeliner sketched on like fight scars,
cinder-goth stockings ritually snagged
with nail files, earring hooks, as if nylon ladders
were lucky charms, thread amulets that coded hope
for mystery, yet escape from harm.
Nor was it taught by my father,
no demonstration or lecture
with crash-test mannequin, puppet-guy stuffed with kettles,
weighted with bricks, bats, axes, rusted anchors
then laid the length of me — no.

My how-to was sleep-born. Schoolgirl, virgin,
one night I birthed a visitation so leaden,
I thought the word *demon*,
a noun that broke the protective caul
of *sensible eldest, doctor's daughter*,
always taught of genes, cells and the formal names
for those warm efflorescing or folded parts —
vulva, breasts, vagina — as a way to stake out safety
around what apple-throated boys had, of late,
just begun to cat-kiss and wolf-croon to —

demon. I woke wedged under a long, cold slab.
It wore a face. In airless dread, I knew
his hair, bones, sex, gender,
and the language clenched between his teeth

as if he bit a steel shank to leave both hands free.
Limbs frozen with muscle atonia,
throat clamped with fear, my single weapon
was awareness: of his contempt, the shadow-lode of hate.

My mind gave just one master class in its own night terror.
Yet as if sleep paralysis ran body-cam, years later,
my reactions spooled exact replicas: no memory error.
That night held no sweet talk, no corsage;
no honeyed wine, no heart's triage.
I lay under a real, flesh man — taker, date rapist —
in proto-narcolepsy: my blank camouflage.
He read that shutdown as his safety. Thought it nothing
to plunge me, plunder me, leave me soft as scooped melon,
tenderised as hyacinth, storm-trodden.
From worse, he spared me.
Again, my last arsenal? Awareness.
I knew him. I can name him. I am witness.

Scapegoat

Once, a stranger on a long coach ride
showed me the birthmark beneath her sleeve.
It looked a little like a red-inked crow
with stooped head and slim, folded tail.

She told me that far back along
the cobweb lines of family history,
was another woman whose honest body
shared the mark and who like a weather vane
was made to spin in the bitter gale of men's fears.

Turn around. Show your skin. Lay your breast bare.

When what they saw
made them weak at the knees
as if thighs, waist, nipples were not soft
but struck like rock against the flint
of their thoughts, they used words
like disguises to distract and dissemble:
that mole, that smatter of freckles were
the bite, the thumbprint of the devil —

her port-wine birthmark
the warm place they might themselves
have stained with a bruising kiss
blunt and crimson as crushed geranium
or blackberries pulped on the tongue, so

Witch, they lied. *Witch.*

Tricks of Trade

Nails and knives for your water?
Livestock and blankets for your daughters?
Three kinds of fever as bloodless slaughter?
Potatoes for your ferns?
Hogs for your forest?
Fish for your whalebone?
A crew for your son?
Handshake for your hongi?
Bibles for your anxieties?
Booze for your braveries?
Spars and timber for joinery?
Muskets for your flax?
Language for your lands?
Treaty for your welfare?
Crown for your trust?

Penny for your thoughts, love?

Genealogy

a tankard slammed like a gavel on wood
               a door wrenched shut like the strike of a fist
the thud of footsteps like blows
               papers screwed up with the fire's snake-hiss

abruptly it starts   in a quarrel

were the words
      you will see me no more   or
I am done with this   [*greed*] [*blindness*] [*injustice*]?
or was it a grieved, silent retraction?

one brother of eight so upset over a father's estate
he moves his family across the world   three months of ocean swell and surge
could seasickness have been a welcome mask   for a man's hurt and anger?

the first night of a new life   asleep on ships' ropes
in a tent made of blankets   which a local
        [Māori man, woman, takatāpui, child? where has
their name slipped, down the scree of time?] helped them to fashion

no record of first impressions   or feeling
but only the near fact it is likely more
[unnamed] Māori [individuals]   built my old-old greats
a drier, roomier raupō hut   away from the swamp eels, floods and mud
        or as *away*
as anyone   nineteenth-century could be
and   how many more
trips and slides   to construct the all-we-knows

until one of those sons had a son   who followed a gold rush
          and who then helped lay
stone upon stone   in the foundations of a school
                which loomed like a
                   [phantom]   in my father's stories
the homesick bullied bright musical unforgettable abandoned
hilarious mischief disappointment searing you-had-to-be-there-days
like a wounded man with other wounded men

as each son made his son   and his son made his son   attend in a line
of honour and tradition   sticklers for formality
          but look that's another story
though always part of this one too
             it all gets very looped and confused
genetic chain of ancestors with similar names
Johns and Johns and Williams and Williams
the Emmas and Emmas and Sarahs and Sarahs

is that one reason why
                    it's easier to recall not the complex, troublesome facts
(the trail of money from mines, mills, ships and coal
          laid down over the names of tribes, rangatira)

but small sharp jolts of love?

                the way the gold-rush son, now a father,
marched the headmaster into the family home
to show him   the weals he had given his son
with a cat o' nine tails   and forbade him
ever to lay hands
              on any of his children again

and the way another son of the gold-rush father
my great-grandfather   helped Hēmi Mātenga
of Delaware Bay fame   fight for his estate,
and Hēmi so grateful   that this great-grandfather's family
was allowed to holiday   along the coast   the very coast
where Hēmi and his wife Hūria rescued men
              from a shipwreck   swimming out
in storm-wildered seas   to grasp a line
      thrown out by the crew,
tie the line   to a large rock
then *with legendary courage* enter
      the water   again   and   again
using another rope linked to the first
      to assist sailors, strangers, to get to shore

their heroic survival, heroic kindness
      a story that makes our family chronicles more comical:

for their holidays at that famous, treacherous bay
my great-grandmother   sewed red linings
into her children's sun caps
      then had to change them to green
            when they 'drew unwelcome attention
from a bull called Sweet William'
      such vivid, trivial facts survive

but can we let these jumbled bright fibres   compassion, fidelity, care
      from small and awkward to large or formal   be the threads of nation
each gentleness done to another
      the rope for a bed, the blanket for a hut, the march of fatherly ire,
lifelines in a shipwreck, arguments for another man in court, the cotton in a cap

        but the coal, the gold, the wars, the land, the whips,
omissions from history are they lies, evasions, age's amnesias,
the inability of children to listen   in time
         the refusal of adults to be perfect museums
              of themselves
is every white genealogy poem   an erasure poem
is every postcolonial poem an erasure poem   will we ever be fair
and true and clear   and where
exactly   do I think
        I am coming from   here?

#notmetoothanks

No, I won't be writing a poem
to celebrate the great poet

while forgoing any
publication fee

because the only night we met
I found his heroic feet

weren't made of gold or music
but all the same tired old shit.

My husband held our firstborn child
while I was introduced to His Big Laurels.

I began to say how his famous lyrics
had altered me when I was young,

walking me into a fresh-peeled world
tingling with rinsed and new-lit skin.

His breath a triple-whisky mist,
he ignored my awe-tied speech

shuffled up and pulled open
the sides of my winter coat.

'Get those titties out right now
and feed that little baby,' he said,

his bloodwebbed eyes rolling back
like a day patient's, half tranquillised.

What could I do with that?
Keep it dry.

Like wit?
Like kindling.

Let the silence speak:
smoke from smouldering peat.

Histology Report

Near Routeburn Station, Glenorchy

Tall, thin thistles and lupins
lined the roadside like blown-glass rods
filled with droplets bright as syrup.

Cars trailed clouds of white dust.
The heat rubbed its cat-barb tongue
in small sharp licks on sunscreen-skipped skin.

We trudged beneath serrated frowns
of watchful mountains;
despite those imperial towers

the boys were stuck in cul-de-sacs of squabbles
or jokes where the punch line was always smut
as if every morning they were caught unawares

by their own forked forms' dawn crow,
had to spend the rest of the day
in a triple double-take —

Hey, hey, I've got a body!

amazed at how it always sprang
to the north of warmth
like a Huntaway nosing the wind.

I'm slowing down now, bored by the bawdy,
my own body conceals confusions,
chains of scrambled instructions,

the space that cupped my children
lined with cells bewildered, proliferate.
Funny not-funny, how the histology reminds me

of my shyest, quietest, kindest great-aunt
who gave me a golden, wind-up watch
almost the moment clockwork was obsolete,

and who couldn't stop cooking for hordes
even when there was no cause or occasion;
still she would labour and bake

bring us scones, gems and cakes
the way an overlooked child gifts, gifts again
pictures of the same scene, in pencil, crayons, paints:

This is us, this is you, that's the sun,
here are the horses, the sheep, the lupins,
and we are walking, walking together,

see, see our smiles inside the clouds of dust,
our hot, tight skins under the lemon sun
that drips like sticky juice on us?

Though I know now she meant love,
how you can't stop it, quite,
once you've got the habit of it

sometimes even if you want to
sometimes even when you know
it can never be fully requited

the world can never love you back enough
to hold you all, on the summer-stung track,
in the hours before the unknown turns known.

The Moth-eyed Steeplechase Horse

At a farm stay in Routeburn
we offer small coins of carrot
to a thoroughbred who lips them up:
our hands held flat as picnic plates
over her paddock fence.

We wait, as if in her amber eyes
we'll find each horse-thought formed
as clear as honeyed cells of wax.

Globed, deep presence,
she takes us in
and we are dreams that flow
easily as bleached driftwood
down a slow river current.

Time piles in cloud towers
as magpie song spirals;
we look away, catch small hot dots
of white, pink, gold
as the sun glints deep in the grass
like dropped wedding rings.

I look back, see the horse
has one dark pupil shaped like a moth,
its scallop-edged wings spreadeagled.
Look at your eye! I want to say,
as if she wears a rare jewel,
yet as our stare expands she seems to see
into each and every human weakness.
I am as thrown as I was, long years ago:

a sadhu, his ochre robes in ropes of rags,
hair twisted in tree-bark strips,
wooden staff in his slim grip,
stoic, singular and alone,
locked his eyes with mine
as I stood there with my palm
clasped inside my husband's
and I felt a catapult of fear:
his receptiveness to pain and drift
against my clinging to love
like a moth's egg to a leaf tip
exposed all that was wrong
and false in us: yes, even the way

I want to hold this morning
under an agapanthus sky
with a gentle, moth-eyed horse
as if the thread of language
could ever weave a hide
against the hook and ache of loss
when we carry it
deep as the mare carries
the sprint, the vault,
in her hocks, her fetlocks.

The Night Shift

I wake on the ward, afloat on ketamine, fentanyl,
see sky-blue morphine swifts roost nearby
in pleated paper thimbles

and some uneasy instinct tugs my gaze
to a scuff mark on the lino floor.
Coal-black, it smoulders. I stall.

A voice reassures me it's just a graze
left by the wheel of some routine machine:
IV, PCA line, heart monitor screen.

Yet as I ease deep-cut core and leaden legs
over the distant side of the tall bed
I can't shake this need to stare

not quite in fear: not quite.

For last night, creatures came.
They arrived *en masse*, nodded, swayed,
pressed into each dimmed cubicle,

their copper eyes bright-candled,
lips pouched over strong, proud teeth,
their heads bowed in silent inspection;

marmalade lions with oxen feet,
crested birds with antlers, candy-pink teats,
hordes crowded, bunched round each bed

as the window in time was fast contracting,
and they wanted us to see before our minds
sealed tough with the fibres of logic, denial.

Their fur packed tight as green florets on catkins.
Their horns, colossal black spikes, gleamed like grand pianos.
Such mass and strength in their embedded weaponry,

yet still, they withheld their crush and maim.

The breath and bunt of their herded skulls
said, *We are the unbroken in you, be unafraid*,
and I saw through the seep of dawn

that soon like guardians they will gather
each one of us, our failing forms absorbed
into their warm, strong-walled veins

until we too watch
each figure on the bed
as something invisible shifts
in the intricate balance of matter and spirit.

So it is awe, not dread, that asks me
to leave the ground undisturbed
where they gathered,
to skirt carefully the sign one left
like a scorched hoof print
as if they had stood in fire
to show they bear time's pyre for us,

our wild sentries, our wild sentries.

If you saw a miracle, would you speak of it?

In a southern valley once, along the green flanks of a river,
we saw a pale creature snagged on brambles and twigs,
the crinkles of its gossamer skin
stitched with sparkles by the needling sun.

Somewhere a frantic music spiralled
from a syrinx smaller than a seedpod.
It roused the creature from its stupor,
a paradox of hobbled grace.

A blue flash
a cool rush
a shuttle shape swept:
silver-throated, eyes black stars,
it fled the daylight's loom.

Dazed, we pushed through trees and bracken.
Neither of us spoke, as if we knew
that if we noosed it too soon
in a rope of language
clear as a ridge named on a map,

others would trace blood cell, talon fibre,
to uncover every instance of its kind,
till each cryptid was strung,
worn limp as the sun-bleached thorax
of a child's lost rainbow-tailed kite;

the symmetry of bones disordered,
the ribbons of its silk-thin hide
flittering like alpine prayer flags

while each creature's complex self
disintegrated into myth.

Wishing he'd declined cocktails, stayed at home to read Janet Frame

People glide the party's rooms
on covert scavenger hunts —
which conversation stows most gold?

His head hums like static on a screen,
feels colossal; it tilts like the badly wired top
of a horse skeleton.

The guests' voices pitch
in daylight robbery
from his small, private stash of self.

His glances at the clock bring strength
like small squares of chocolate
smuggle-eaten inside the pantry.

When the hostess lies down
beneath rain-damp white roses
that glow, small night lamps,

he slips free into skinny streets,
the trees like cut-outs
stapled to the dark.

Traffic pours along; a liquid metal
reminding him every decade
holds manipulations

almost too terrifying
to admit.
He hurries home

to where a silence hangs
plump, wine-heady, sweet
as late wasp-kissed blackberries

and soon a cube of light hovers
a mandala between his eyes
with the after-brilliance

from a turned end-page.

Stranded

Down in the city river's rushing roil
stalled by the slope and shallows of the weir
a brown trout is almost at a swim-still.
It shifts the rudder of itself
to and fro just a little;
local children lean over the bridge rail
to call, 'It's a frozen fish!'
As it tilts, turns and tilts and turns
but still can't fight its way upstream
one girl sings high, 'It's melting!'

We're hypnotised by this live, brown topaz
that glints flexuous under the water's skin,
wish we could clamber down, wade out with a net,
scoop then free it to the deep cascade
near the river's muddy northern bank.

The children yell, 'Look *beside* you! Swim that way!'
as they would to the innocent in a pantomime
then, as winter dusk sifts down its fine grey ice,
'How now brown trout? Oh, sad. That's how,'
and 'Ah well, poor fish, can't be helped,'
while the city's traffic swells, jolts us
from the trance where we might rescue a fish
to find it can speak in gold bullion,
or shimmy out of its sequined sheath,
some fey bewitchment lifted
at the quickening contact
of *our surplus love* …

The image of it stalled yet fighting
locks in my head for days, insistent glitch,
latent anxiety of an undelivered promise;
which might be why, mid-week,
when we see a young man lean in despair
against an overbridge, hunched and bowed
straining against a foe, vertigo, or a voice
that even his earbuds' jazz won't blank,
we're out of the car, across the street,
through the night frost, calling, 'Can we help you?'
Then closer, 'Is there anyone we can phone?'
My hand lifts to his shoulder through the dark
as we see the cars far below, see his body quiver
with the hammer of his pulse.

His abrupt flinch from contact,
the woman running over the road
shouting, 'Josie! It's all right, I know Josie.
Josie, stop. You know me. You know me …'
discharges us from the fable
where at the strength of someone's need
our poor mortal powers transform
to make us saviours.

What else have we so sorely misread?
Back in the car, the radio knows.
It spills an era's doublespeak,
pours vortex from its maw.

'Just the plain truth, as only a liar can tell it'

This is just to say
I found the chocolate you hid
at my request
to save me from myself

it was stashed behind my Mansfield books
on the hallway bookshelf
the age-scuffed chunks so sweet
yet so stale

they left me hankering
for something more substantial
so like a kitchen maid who longs
to scry courage or counsel

from almanac or Bible
I flipped pages to all the indices
in Katherine's notebooks and *Collected Letters*
to follow where her leaf-runes led me:

'I have too great an appetite for the real thing
to be put off with pretty kickshaws.'

'When I kissed you did we wake?'

'the boats, with long fans of light, go dancing by'

'— and all this love and joy that fights for outlet —
and all this life drying up, like milk, in an old breast —'

From thinnest nick to crippling strike
the heart's every blow
marked with the glance
of a polished steel tip

its glint ambiguous
as teeth bared
at the edge of the firelight's
pas de chat.

Sempre marcatissimo

At not-quite-one minute into Tchaikovsky's *Serenade for Strings*,
when the cellos and the bass sound like sad doors slowly opened
on a figure cut from dusk as he trudges up our concrete steps,
scent of Hibitane, black coffee, mint, floating in with his shadow,
some instrument in my chest lifts; for like flickering sight, my father's ghost
saccades there, between notes that pulse with rose and copper wings.

He waits, listens, winces at the accurate bow strikes,
the double-stops, the mountainous chordal forms,
as if he too recalls them from the tiny cassette deck he gave me.
They pierce him with all the life he has not led
away from that old house, where, like the flanks
of wolfish military dogs, sea fog pressed against its walls,
or ramshackle tanks of winter rain rumbled above the garden's drabs.

In the wide front hallway, in memory, he wrenches off his work tie
as if I've interrupted him punishing himself
and he's furious he hasn't even fucking found
the chance to get that done; the pallor of his face a colour
I only ever see in certain strangers, in years to come,
when I guess correctly they are hospital physicians
grey from nights on call and draining, daily rounds.

The violins weave and tighten the lariat of self-flagellation,
the conviction that for all his small-hour striving
to keep patients' lives above the rising, mortal waters,
he never fully earned his army-doctor father's
exacting, formal love;
yet when the strings plunge into the allegro
at only three minutes fifteen seconds
his presence has already diminished

so I play and replay the opening bars,
to hold him here, like dammed-back tears,
while I sit as hypnotised as a child
with a banded sphinx moth in a lidded jar:
transfixed by its ardent battering.

Dreams are the dark glasses and heatproof shell the mind wears when the truth is a hot, burning ball of plasma and at least sixty-seven known elements

She tells him of how last night she woke,
sleep peeled off as easily as damp Band-Aids,
so the world's latest sadness, the one like glinting, molten tar
stung in the midnight air and even when
sleep's weather at last crept back into her head,
knowledge of the damage bulked there
like some security guard on sombre vigil in the dark;
and soon, in the narrow alleyways of uneasy dreams,
that blue devil morphed, took the form
of bizarre, misshapen, fly-black beetles that scavenged
into the Kindness Cakes someone had baked,
before they scurried under another pan named the Forgiveness Dish.
'Sad beetles,' she repeated. 'All the grief was there —
but as beetles, burrowing.'

And the man she loved said — mouth just shy
of mournfulness — 'Did you know, there is actually
a kind of beetle that can make its own way
through the digestive tract of a frog,
then climb right out, still alive?'

At first, she could have cried, for how entirely
this seemed to miss the point — but you know,
love is its own strangely layered card game,
so she pulled out another insect fact
like a two-faced joker that switches suits
as often as a chorus extra sheds costumes in a musical,
and asked, 'What about the golden tortoise beetle,
Charidotella sexpunctata? Have you ever heard of that?

It looks like a tiny mechanical gadget,
parts fourteen carat, parts completely see-through.
Often as small as a drawing pin,
it levitates like a helicopter,
polished mirror-gold,
gleaming like new wedding rings.'

'Huh,' he said. 'Hmm,' she nodded.

And they both watched and waited
as if all the latest sadness
in its glistening black jackets
would simply scroll itself away.

An Abraham Darby Rose

My rose stands in for a young, fledged love
with its peach-toned ruffles

and the peppery, specked
green paddles of its leaves

that steer it steady through
the choppy wash of light

as money spiders, tiny sentient comets,
glitter across it,

aphids suckle like blood-drunken fleas
at buds pink as shorn underfleece,

and a rain-grey mouse
noses up for cover

below the billowing shawl
of one bloom's blowsy awning.

When our first child left home
I sought out this hardy shrub-rose:

carried its cloth-swaddled roots
to the soil's quiet crib,

whispered nonsense nothings to it
as it bowed its drowsy coral head

and seemed, if not to listen,
not to not-listen,

while my mind finned down
to till for the why of things,

winnowing for the difference
between neurons and ocelli,

consciousness and plant vision,
our selves and the world that senses us,

even if it doesn't answer
nor understand, as I barely do,

our arrivals, departures,
the dorsal-fin-shaped thorns that rise

in the under-swim of the mind
as I try to absorb, through separation's long sting,

both the wisdom of physics
and some mystic, self-help spin

insistent, each one, that time
is a relative illusion.

The Lie's Version

Born in a rush of heat
and racing heart beat

son of fear
daughter of shame

bare as my own cheek
and slippery as an eel

I lay between my parents
like a tadpole, all tail,

where my father tightened his grip
quick as lick a dish

and my mother suckled me
on the sly-milk of language.

NOTES & ACKNOWLEDGEMENTS

The epigraph appears in James Orchard Halliwell (ed.), *The Early Naval Ballads of England,* Volume 2, Issue 2 (London: Percy Society, 1841). The full ditty runs: 'Liar, liar, lick spit / Turn about the candlestick. / What's good for liar? / Brimstone and fire.' The title of this collection adds an extra comma.

'False Confession': Kurdish poet İlhan Sami Çomak has been unlawfully imprisoned in Turkey since 1994.

The quotation in 'Porky' comes from Joseph Brodsky, 'Less Than One' (1976), *Less Than One: Selected Essays* (Toronto: Farrar, Straus & Giroux, 1986).

'In the nodding grass below the cat's-cradle clothesline, my hand an open perch': The form here is borrowed from Ella Frears' 'desire line' series in *The Poetry Review* (Autumn 2023), with the poet's consent. Thank you to Ella Frears for her generous response to a random, enthusiastic Instagram message.

'A Very *Perhaps* Man': This poem grew out of one of the surreal options ('little elegant afternoons') offered as an answer to a question in my Duolingo Spanish practice. It was far more interesting than the right answer.

'Torque/Talk': I'd like to acknowledge poets Jasmine Gallagher and Jeanann Verlee for their inspirational use of footnotes in some of their poetry. Reading their work helped me to find the form to write about the experience recorded here.

'&': This poem was written in subconscious dialogue with a wonderful poem by Poppy Haynes. Poppy's poem also features ampersands and knots. When I remembered, much after the fact, that the poems shared a language, I wondered whether unconscious echoes of sources/literary influences like this weren't only a sign of correspondence and affection, but also another kind of lie: like faulty memory.

'Wishing he'd declined cocktails, stayed at home to read Janet Frame': This poem arose from re-reading Janet Frame's *The Edge of the Alphabet* after a gap of about 25 years. I set myself a pastiche exercise: a fan letter, really, sent across time. Two phrases in particular from the novel are echoed here: 'Now the moments hanging ripe, transparent like red currants' and 'the weapons of people … their secret robberies from themselves …' See Janet Frame, *The Edge of the Alphabet* (Christchurch: Pegasus Press, 1962).

'Stranded': Line 27 quotes John Berryman's 'Dream Song 155'.

'Found': After Antony Gormley's cast-iron sculpture *Found*, often called the Iron Baby, exhibited at the Foundling Museum, London.

'Genealogy': This poem springs from June E. Neale's booklet *Neale Family History* (Nelson: 1974). The form is indebted to 'Settlers' by Fleur Adcock, from *The Inner Harbour* (London: Oxford University Press, 1979).

'Just the plain truth as only a liar could tell it': The title is a line from Katherine Mansfield's short story 'A Married Man's Story'. The poem quotes from Vincent O'Sullivan and Margaret Scott (eds), *The Collected Letters of Katherine Mansfield*, Volumes 1, 3 and 5 (Oxford: Oxford University Press, 1984, 1987 and 2008).

'The Lie's Version': The line 'quick as lick a dish' borrows another saying about lies: 'liar, liar, lick-dish', which, apparently, dates from as early as the 1400s. See Cara Giaimo, 'All the Lies about the Origins of "Liar, Liar, Pants on Fire"', *Atlas Obscura* (18 September 2017, www.atlasobscura.com/articles/liar-liar-pants-on-fire-origin-phrase-history).

*

Many thanks to the editors and publishers of the following publications, where some of these poems (or earlier versions) originally appeared, or are forthcoming: *adda: Remember to Rest*, Issue 2, Commonwealth Writers' Foundation (UK); *a fine line*; *And We Pass Through* (UK); *At the Bay | I Te Kokoru*, Phantom Billsticker Poster Series; *Bear Review* (US); *Eight Poems 2021* (Pear Tree Press); *Episteme Annual Magazine* (India); *Ink Sweat & Tears* (UK); *Landfall*; the *New Zealand Listener*; *London Grip* (UK); *Mayhem*; the New Zealand Poet Laureate blog; NZ Poetry Shelf; *Otago Daily Times*; *Panoplyzine* (US); *Remake*; *Shenandoah* (US); *Snow Crow: Bath Flash Fiction Volume Six* (Ad Hoc Fiction, UK); *Stasis Journal*; *Sweet Mammalian*; *The Spinoff*; and the Verb Wellington website.

Thank you to the judges who selected these poems (or earlier versions of them) for the following competitions: 'Pandora First Gets Feminism' was longlisted in the February 2021 Bath Flash Fiction Award (UK). 'Genealogy' was shortlisted for the *Ink Sweat & Tears* 'Pick of the Month' for May 2023 (UK). '⌘S' was joint winner of the Manhire Challenge, a NZSA Wellington competition for National Poetry Day in 2023. 'An Abraham Darby Rose', under the title 'A David Austin Rose', won the published poets section of the Robert Burns Poetry Competition 2023. 'Scapegoat' was shortlisted by Liz Berry for the Bridport Prize (UK), October 2024.

Thank you to Creative New Zealand for generous financial support through a 2020/21 Arts Grant.

It feels as if there has been not only a village, but a citadel, helping to raise this book. I want to thank its population:

Anna Hodge, for editing both this collection and *To the Occupant*: thank you for your patience, energy and your laser-beam eyes. Sue Wootton, for grant application support early in a busy new job and for astute editorial attention to the final collection.

The Black's Road Poetry Workshop for exacting and enthusiastic poetry talk: Megan Kitching, Nicola Thorstensen, Carolyn McCurdie and Jonathan Cweorth.

Majella Cullinane, my Messenger Cheerleader, and Vanessa Manhire, for 'twitch and bitch'.

Dunedin/Ōtepoti and Otago literary community friends: so many of you, including book clubbers, but Michael Harlow, Bronwyn Wylie-Gibb, Louise Wallace, Michelle Elvy and Penelope Todd have loaned their ears most often.

Thanks and love to my family: the WhatsApp 'Aunt Sally Ladies', Barbara Else and Sarah Easton Neale; and Chris Else, my stepfather; all three for vital conversations. My husband, Danny Baillie, for unfailing support and rigorous, sceptical discussions about everything under and over the sun. Our children, Abe and Zac Baillie, for who they are and everything they teach us. And to my father, Jim Neale, who gave me so much.

Published by Otago University Press
Te Whare Tā o Ōtākou Whakaihu Waka
533 Castle Street
Dunedin, New Zealand
university.press@otago.ac.nz
www.oup.nz

First published 2024
Copyright © Emma Neale

The moral rights of the author have been asserted.
ISBN 978-1-99-004888-3

A catalogue record for this book is available from the National Library of New Zealand. This book is copyright. Except for the purpose of fair review, no part may be stored or transmitted in any form or by any means, electronic or mechanical, including recording or storage in any information retrieval system, without permission in writing from the publishers. No reproduction may be made, whether by photocopying or by any other means, unless a licence has been obtained from the publisher.

Editor: Anna Hodge
Design/layout: Fiona Moffat

Front cover: Laura Williams, *New Berlin Ether II*, 2023, (detail), acrylic on canvas, 50 x 55 x 3mm. Courtesy of the artist and Laree Payne Gallery

Printed in New Zealand by Ligare